WRITING FOR SOCIAL MEDIA

BCS, THE CHARTERED INSTITUTE FOR IT

BCS, The Chartered Institute for IT, is committed to making IT good for society. We use the power of our network to bring about positive, tangible change. We champion the global IT profession and the interests of individuals, engaged in that profession, for the benefit of all.

Exchanging IT expertise and knowledge

The Institute fosters links between experts from industry, academia and business to promote new thinking, education and knowledge sharing.

Supporting practitioners

Through continuing professional development and a series of respected IT qualifications, the Institute seeks to promote professional practice tuned to the demands of business. It provides practical support and information services to its members and volunteer communities around the world.

Setting standards and frameworks

The Institute collaborates with government, industry and relevant bodies to establish good working practices, codes of conduct, skills frameworks and common standards. It also offers a range of consultancy services to employers to help them adopt best practice.

Become a member

Over 70,000 people including students, teachers, professionals and practitioners enjoy the benefits of BCS membership. These include access to an international community, invitations to roster of local and national events, career development tools and a quarterly thought-leadership magazine. Visit www.bcs.org/membership to find out more.

Further Information
BCS, The Chartered Institute for IT,
First Floor, Block D,
North Star House, North Star Avenue,
Swindon, SN2 1FA, United Kingdom.
T +44 (0) 1793 417 424
F +44 (0) 1793 417 444
(Monday to Friday, 09:00 to 17:00 UK time)

www.bcs.org/contact

http://shop.bcs.org/

WRITING FOR SOCIAL MEDIA

Carrie Marshall

The right of Carrie Marshall to be identified as author of this work has been asserted by her in accordance with sections 77 and 78 of the Copyright, Designs and Patents Act 1988.

Published by BCS Learning & Development Ltd, a wholly owned subsidiary of BCS, The Chartered Institute for IT, First Floor, Block D, North Star House, North Star Avenue, Swindon, SN2 1FA, UK.
www.bcs.org

PDF ISBN: 978-1-78017-4518
ePUB ISBN: 978-1-78017-4525
Kindle ISBN: 978-1-78017-4532
Paperback ISBN: 978-1-78017-4501

Ebook available

British Cataloguing in Publication Data.
A CIP catalogue record for this book is available at the British Library.

Disclaimer:
The views expressed in this book are of the author(s) and do not necessarily reflect the views of the Institute or BCS Learning & Development Ltd except where explicitly stated as such. Although every care has been taken by the authors and BCS Learning & Development Ltd in the preparation of the publication, no warranty is given by the authors or BCS Learning & Development Ltd as publisher as to the accuracy or completeness of the information contained within it and neither the authors nor BCS Learning & Development Ltd shall be responsible or liable for any loss or damage whatsoever arising by virtue of such information or any instructions or advice contained within this publication or by any of the aforementioned.

Publisher's acknowledgements
Reviewers: Oliver Lindberg and Jemma Davis
Publisher: Ian Borthwick
Commissioning Editor: Rebecca Youé
Production Manager: Florence Leroy
Project Manager: Sunrise Setting Ltd
Cover work: Alex Wright
Picture credits: Shutterstock/Quang Ho
Typeset by Lapiz Digital Services, Chennai, India.

CONTENTS

AUTHOR

Carrie Marshall is a journalist, copywriter, ghostwriter and broadcaster from Glasgow. A professional writer for 20 years, she has written thousands of features, columns, reviews and news stories for a huge range of magazines, newspapers, websites and trade publications. As a copywriter she has crafted copy for some of the biggest names in the technology, retail, audio and finance industries, and as a novelist she sold enough copies of her self-published debut to buy a car. Not a great car, but still: a car! Under various names, Carrie has written 11 non-fiction books, co-written six more and co-written a six-part BBC Radio 2 documentary series. She blogs at bigmouthstrikesagain.com and tweets as @carrieinglasgow.

PREFACE

It's a whole new world. Most of us carry incredibly powerful internet-connected devices in our pockets or bags all the time, and those devices are transforming the way we live, work and play.

One of the most dramatic transformations is the rise of social media, which is expected to reach one-third of the entire population of Earth by 2020.[1] In 2017, 99 per cent of UK 16–24-year-olds said they had used social media in the previous week, with most saying they used it for an hour a day (Deloitte 2017).

In this book you will discover the key social media services you need to know about, who uses them and how best to reach your customers and potential customers through engaging writing on social media. You'll also discover the many traps firms can fall into, and how to avoid them.

WHAT THIS BOOK WILL COVER

In **Chapter 1** you'll discover that social media is much more than Facebook and Twitter.

In **Chapter 2** you'll learn the importance of having a social media strategy, and the dangers of not having a strategy at all.

---

[1] https://www.statista.com/topics/1164/social-networks/

In **Chapter 3** we'll investigate the different demographics of the key social media services.

In **Chapter 4** you'll consider the importance of having a brand persona and how to integrate it with your existing marketing and customer service.

In **Chapter 5** you'll discover how to communicate big ideas when you are limited to very small amounts of text or media, and in **Chapter 6** you'll examine the best ways to write content for the major social media platforms.

Chapter 7 explores shareability: what makes some content go viral and other content sink like a stone?

Chapter 8 analyses some major social media mistakes and what we can learn from them.

Chapter 9 is all about the timing: posts do better at some times than at others.

Chapter 10 explores the issues of posting content to platforms where audiences seem desperate to be offended, and **Chapter 11** identifies strategies for dealing with the most offensive social media users of all.

Chapter 12 explores the various technological tools you can use to manage your social media activity. And in the **Appendix**, we'll look at the numbers: what social media platforms are people really using?

1   WHAT IS SOCIAL MEDIA?

Social media is a broader category than many people realise. The big names such as Facebook, Twitter and Instagram are there, of course. But there are many more, often with little in common other than being used by a community of people. Wikipedia is social media: its content is created by lots of individual users. The Audi Owners' Club Forum is social media. The controversial discussion site Reddit is social media, as is the Q&A site Quora. All kinds of businesses now have a social media element: for example, sporting brands' sites enable customers to compare their personal bests with others; many businesses' websites have blogs where senior figures let loose; and media sites enable readers to comment on articles.

If the site enables users to create or share content or network with other people, it's social media.

WHAT DO BUSINESSES DO ON SOCIAL MEDIA?

Social media is not just where we share photos or argue on Twitter. It's where businesses advertise – Facebook alone has more than 50 million small businesses using Facebook Pages to connect with their customers – and it's where their customers expect them to be: 95 per cent of online adults aged 18 to 30 will follow a brand on social media (Leslie 2018).

It drives sales. *The Drum* reported that by 2015, Facebook was influencing 52 per cent of consumers' spending, both on the internet and in bricks and mortar shops (McCarthy 2015).

It's where customers complain. *Time* magazine reported in 2017 that one retailer, Target in the US, was fielding 3,500 tweets and direct messages every month (Stainmetz 2017). Social media is also where mishandled complaints can go badly wrong, with 60 per cent of consumers saying they would take 'unpleasant actions' to express their dissatisfaction with companies online (Petersen 2015).

It's where fashion lives and dies, where products can be funded overnight, where employers seek new staff and where businesses give their staid old image a funky new makeover.

It's somewhere your business probably needs to be.

CH-CH-CH CHANGES

The rise of social media has had some interesting consequences, both good and bad. The rise of user reviews has been a blessing and a curse. For some industries, such as the hospitality industry, the benefits of word of mouth marketing have been eclipsed by a plague of malicious comments on travel and restaurant guides. And for consumers, it often means wading through plausible-looking but utterly fake reviews on big retailers' websites.

It has enabled companies to respond more quickly to their customers, but that just means customers expect ever faster responses: 53 per cent of Twitter users expect firms to respond to them within the hour, and they get publicly angry if firms don't (Vaughan 2017).

For many organisations, it's replaced the telephone call as the primary method of customer or client communication, but for others it's also enabled critics, the perpetually outraged and all kinds of time wasters to cause more trouble than ever before.

How do you make it work for your business?

HOW TO BECOME A SOCIAL MEDIA MOGUL

The first step is to identify which social networks are right for your business. Would a Facebook presence bring people through the door or help to sell products, or is the Twitter crowd a better demographic? If you're selling parts for Audis, would your time be better spent on focused sites such as the Audi Owners' Forum than on one of the big social networks? Would social media work as a marketing tool, or is it best suited to brand awareness and perhaps hiring new people? Can it bring you closer to your customers in a cost-effective way?

Armed with that knowledge, you can then create content for your chosen network or networks: shareable content to build your brand; adverts that encourage people not just to click but to hand over their credit cards; long-form articles establishing you as an expert in your field; blog posts to delight your existing customers and attract new ones too.

Over the coming chapters you will discover the dos and don'ts of writing for social media. We won't just cover the nuts and bolts of what to do where and how to craft compelling copy, we'll also look at the wider context: what encourages people to share businesses' content? How do you ensure you don't fall foul of the perpetual outrage machine that even the big brands sometimes underestimate?

In this book, I will tell you what you actually need to know, and I'll do it without overselling and overhyping things like the self-proclaimed 'thought leaders' of social media.

In fact, that is the first tip. Don't let anybody in your organisation call themselves a thought leader.

SOCIAL MEDIA: THE SKILLS THAT MATTER

The mechanics of social media posting, scheduling and analytics are no more complicated than any basic function built around using software: it's not hard, and it doesn't take long to learn.

The skills that matter most are communication skills and a good understanding of your business's brand pillars. Think public relations or communications, not advertising; social media is a conversation, not a broadcast. A thick skin is often helpful, especially in business sectors that attract a lot of criticism such as retail or transport, and an eye to the future is invaluable: being able to see what's coming next means you're not stuck posting to MySpace, when everybody's jumped ship to Facebook.

KEY TAKEAWAYS

- Social media is not just Facebook and Twitter. It's anywhere users create and share content.

- For many customers, social media is their favoured way to contact businesses.

- Unfortunately, social media empowers critics as well as customers.

- Don't call yourself a thought leader.

2 KNOW WHAT YOU WANT TO ACHIEVE

In many respects, 'you need to be on social media' is today's version of the 1990s mantra 'you need to have a website', and, like those faraway days, it's resulted in an awful lot of organisations spending an awful lot of money on things that are, well, awful.

Do you remember the days of businesses offering 20 screens of Flash-heavy animations about their vision, but neglecting to include their phone number? A lot of companies' social media presences are just like that.

That's because some businesses simply follow the latest trends and rush into things without actually working out what they want to achieve. It's the investment equivalent of driving around aimlessly in a place you don't know in the hope that somehow you'll end up where you want to be. Even if you do get there, it will be by luck rather than judgement and you will have wasted a lot of petrol.

As we have already discovered, there are multiple reasons why a business might be on social media. For your social media to be successful, those reasons need to be SMART.

SMART THINKING

I try to steer clear of acronyms, but I will make an exception for our old friend SMART. **Specific**, **Measurable**, **Achievable**, **Realistic** and **Timely** objectives enable you to identify exactly what you want to achieve, how you're going to know if you've achieved it or not, and when you expect to have achieved it by.

We apply SMART decision making to all kinds of investment decisions. We plan and measure our marketing efforts, our investment in training, our investments in new hardware or software – and we can do exactly the same with social media.

For example, if you see social media primarily as a marketing tool, you can apply SMART thinking to that. If the goal is to increase sales: by how much? In which particular region or product sector?

Or, if you see social media as a customer support channel, you might have a target of reducing customers' wait time between initial contact and their problem being resolved, or increasing the average number of customers helped by each operator. Again, you can quantify and monitor that.

Even fairly vague-sounding goals can be quantified and monitored. For example, you can measure customer satisfaction or brand awareness with surveys.

Of course, you do not need to have specific goals in order to be on social media. But you should if you're planning to invest time and money in it.

FIND THE WHY

The key here is to find the why: why are you on social media? If a company can't answer with a straightforward reply, that company is probably wasting its time and quite possibly a whole bunch of money too.

As we'll discover throughout this book, social media is a serious business tool – but without direction and SMART thinking, it can be a serious waste of time and money.

CURB YOUR ENTHUSIASM

It's important to have realistic expectations of your social media activity. If your organisation is expecting a huge and immediate rise in sales or profitability as a result of social media, the adventure is probably going to end in tears. Despite the apparent fast-paced nature of social media, it's a slower, more organic media than other forms of media, best suited to brand awareness and engagement. It's a marathon, not a sprint.

KEY TAKEAWAYS

- Social media without a strategy may well be a waste of time and money.
- Find the why: why do you need to be on social media?
- Set specific, measurable goals wherever you can.
- Social media is more about awareness and engagement than the hard sell.
- Social media is a marathon, not a sprint.

3 DIFFERENT STROKES FOR DIFFERENT FOLKS

Different social media platforms have different audiences, and that affects your writing: there's a world of difference between the young people of Tumblr and the older executives of LinkedIn. There are also differences in how those audiences access their favoured social media services, and the devices they access them on. You will also find some differences from country to country, although such differences are usually relatively minor. For example, while users in the West sometimes found Twitter's original 140-character limit frustrating, users in countries such as China didn't; their language enabled them to express much more with fewer characters.

The main difference in language is in tone and content. LinkedIn users are not big fans of frivolity; Instagram isn't really a place for being serious. Twitter can help warn you of incoming public relations (PR) problems – although its echo chamber effect can make problems look bigger than they actually are – or be a forum for customer service or amusing brand awareness campaigns. Pinterest is a good place to market small, design-focused firms (and sadly, a good place for large, money-focused firms to steal those small firms' ideas). And Facebook wants to be all things to all men and women.

So, how do you decide which social network or networks are best for your brand or business? It's all in the demographics. If you want to reach white collar job-hunters and affluent employers, for example, then LinkedIn is the place to be. If you're promoting products to the widest possible audience, Facebook may be your new best friend. You don't have to be on every conceivable social network to get results, and it's often better to focus your efforts on a small number of platforms.

With a little bit of help from the Pew Research Center's excellent Social Media Study,[2] let's look at the key characteristics of each major social network. As most of the English language social networks are based in the US, their biggest markets are often there too and, as a result, most stats about social media usage tend to be very US-focused. However, the breakdowns and trends are remarkably similar everywhere.

WHO'S ON FACEBOOK?

Facebook is the 500-pound gorilla of social networking, with more than a billion daily users. It's also the easiest social network to study thanks to its Audience Insights tool, which you can use to find out exactly who's online where (https://www.facebook.com/ads/audience-insights).

According to Facebook, its UK demographics break down like this:

> **Gender:** 52 per cent women, 48 per cent men
>
> **Education:** 65 per cent university level, 6 per cent post-graduate, 29 per cent high school
>
> **Job title:** Facebook provides a big breakdown on this, but the biggest numbers are for people in sales (36 per cent), admin (28 per cent) and management (18 per cent).[3]

You can break these statistics down in all kinds of fun ways with the Audience Insights tool; so, for example, you can limit your search to people in the agriculture industry or aviation.

---

[2] The figures quoted here are from the 2018 Pew Research Center's study, but have been pretty consistent for several years. See http://www.pewinternet.org/2018/03/01/social-media-use-in-2018/ and http://www.pewinternet.org/fact-sheet/social-media/

[3] Although, note that job titles on Facebook can be difficult to categorise in this way as the 'job title' field is a free text field, meaning results can be ambiguous.

Globally, Facebook is used by 83 per cent of women and 75 per cent of men who have internet access. It reaches 88 per cent of 18–29-year-olds, 84 per cent of 30–49-year-olds, 72 per cent of 50–64-year-olds and 62 per cent of those over 65 (Brennan 2017).

WHO'S ON LINKEDIN?

Daily user numbers are not available for LinkedIn, but the most recent statistics at the time of writing show 467 million registered members, a quarter of those in the US and just over 20 million in the UK. Its business focus makes it much more urban than other networks – 34 per cent of the urban audience, but 18 per cent of the rural one – and more educated than Twitter or Instagram, with 50 per cent of users having graduated from further education. Its audience is better off too: 45 per cent of adults earning over $75,000 pa use LinkedIn.[4]

LinkedIn provides another useful statistic: in the US, 35 per cent of unemployed adults and 17 per cent of employed adults use the service.

WHO'S ON INSTAGRAM?

Instagram – which is owned by Facebook – skews younger and has a smaller user base, although at 600 million active users it's still huge. Where Facebook reaches all demographics equally, Instagram is more urban (39 per cent urban users compared to 28 per cent suburban and 31 per cent rural), much more popular among women (38 per cent of women with internet access compared to 26 per cent of men) and much more youthful (reaching 59 per cent of 18–29-year-olds, but just 8 per cent of the over-65 internet audience). Women are the dominant gender in each age group.

---

[4] See note 2.

WHO'S ON TWITTER?

Twitter's become quite a big deal for customer service, but it doesn't reach the big numbers that Facebook does. It's more cagey about numbers too. The tech site Recode.net estimated 157 million active daily users in 2017 (Wagner 2017), but that number includes large numbers of bots. Bots are automated Twitter accounts and an ongoing headache for the service alongside fake followers, which can be bought by the thousand for around £20. That makes it exceptionally difficult to work out how many real human beings are on Twitter and how many of those human beings are actually interacting with the accounts they follow.

The numbers show that in the US, Twitter reaches 24 per cent of online men and 25 per cent of women, that its reach is identical in urban, suburban and rural areas, and that once again it skews younger than Facebook: it reaches 36 per cent of 18–29-year-olds, 23 per cent of 30–49-year-olds, 21 per cent of 50–64-year-olds and 10 per cent of the over-65s.

WHO'S ON PINTEREST?

The photo-pinning site doesn't immediately spring to mind when you consider social media, but it's an important site for designers and the fashion business and for a wide range of artistic businesses including home decoration and improvements, wedding planners, gifts and so on. It skews very female (45 per cent of women but just 17 per cent of men) and fairly young, reaching 36 per cent of 18–29-year-olds, 34 per cent of 30–49-year-olds, 28 per cent of the over-50s and 16 per cent of the over-60s.[5]

The suburban market is the biggie here: 34 per cent, compared to 30 per cent of the urban audience and 25 per cent of the rural one. That represents a minor change from before, where

---

[5] See note 2.

the rural audience accounted for the biggest share of Pinterest users.

WHO USES INSTANT MESSAGING APPS?

The Sproutsocial.com website, which makes social media marketing tools, collated Pew's figures on leading messaging apps such as Kik and WhatsApp to discover that they reached 31 per cent of men and 27 per cent of women (York 2017). The demographics are much younger than for other social media: 42 per cent of 18–29-year-olds, 29 per cent of the over-30s and 19 per cent of over-50s. You can deduce popularity among current students and recently graduated students by the comparatively high levels of education and low levels of income among users of the services: just 28 per cent of users earning over $50,000 use the big messaging apps.

WHO'S ON SNAPCHAT?

Sproutsocial.com also looked at so-called auto-delete apps, which enable users to send messages that only last for a short time. They are hugely popular among younger internet users, with SnapChat alone boasting over 160 million users. It and its imitators reach 56 per cent of 18–29-year-olds but just 9 per cent of the over-50s.

A new category is the rise of anonymous chat apps, such as Whisper, which enable users to stay anonymous in group conversations. They are very much a niche at the time of writing, reaching just 5 per cent of online men and 7 per cent of online women and nobody over 50.

WHO'S DOING IT EVERY DAY?

One of the most important questions to ask about a social network isn't just how many people use it, but how often.

For example, while 29 per cent of adults use LinkedIn, they don't do so every day. The number for that group is just 18 per cent.

As you might expect, messaging apps are the most likely to be used daily – although you might be surprised to discover that the real-time feed of Twitter is not a daily habit for everybody. For the big-name social media platforms, the number of people who say they use the services daily are:

- Facebook: 76 per cent
- Instagram: 51 per cent
- Twitter: 42 per cent
- Pinterest: 25 per cent
- LinkedIn: 18 per cent

DON'T FORGET THE FOCUSED SITES

I mentioned the Audi Owners' Club Forum in Chapter 1, and such sites can be really important. One of the great things about social media is that it enables people with very specific interests to get together, either on stand-alone websites or on subsections of big media platforms such as Reddit's subreddits or Facebook's user groups. And that can be a great opportunity for businesses who cater for people with those very specific interests.

For example, a wig maker might want to participate in forums dedicated to hair loss, to cosplay (costume play, something that's really popular among sci-fi and fantasy fans) or to transgender people. A firm making scenery might get involved in sites devoted to plastic modelling or classic train sets. A company making or selling high-performance graphics cards might hang around sites for serious gamers, or for people mining cryptocurrencies such as Bitcoin, or for 3D graphics artists, or for video editors.

In each of these cases, running in with all marketing guns blazing is likely to be counter-productive, but the goodwill generated by being an active and valuable member of a particular community can often deliver direct and indirect results such as sales or word of mouth recommendations. It doesn't take a lot of effort or expense to do, either.

KEY TAKEAWAYS

- Different networks have different audiences with differing expectations and behaviours, and that means you need to write differently.

- On Twitter, beware the bots: fake and automated accounts are an ongoing headache.

- Not all networks are used daily. Some, such as LinkedIn, are less frequent destinations.

- Don't forget about niche communities.

4   WHO ARE YOU?

In 2014, a Twitter user called Immy 'Badman' Bugti sent a message to the retailer Argos via Twitter. Frustrated by shortages of PS4 games consoles in Manchester, Bugti wrote:

> YO wen u getting da ps4 tings in moss side? Ain't waitin no more. Plus da asian guy whu works dere got bare attitude #wasteman

The Argos Helpers account promptly replied:

> Safe badman, we gettin sum more PS4 tings in wivin da next week y'get me. Soz bout da attitude, probz avin a bad day yo.[6]

The exchange went viral, as have many such exchanges: firms such as Virgin Trains, Greggs, Waterstones, Tesco and many more have briefly become social media stars for their sassy replies, tweets that may have helped with the organisations' online images.

It's not all sunshine, flowers and impressed online audiences, though. Argos's response was seen as racist and patronising by some, and in January 2018 Virgin Trains 'apologised unreservedly' for a sexist response to a passenger complaint. When Emily Cole tweeted about being called 'honey' by a member of staff, Virgin Trains East Coast asked her: 'Would you prefer "pet" or "love" next time?'[7] And when Richard Branson

---

[6] See http://www.itv.com/news/2014-03-10/safe-badman-argos-twitter-exchange-wins-thousands-of-fans/

[7] See https://www.dailyrecord.co.uk/news/uk-world-news/would-you-prefer-pet-love-11784537

posted that Virgin wanted to help save the environment, it was comedian Frankie Boyle's response that got the traffic and the online attention: 'You own an airline, you mad @@@@!'[8]

Every brand needs an online persona, but as the above examples prove, it can be difficult to get it right.

PICKING YOUR PERSONA

Your brand persona may already exist, especially if you are in an established firm or larger organisation where marketing is handled by dedicated in-house teams or outside agencies. But sometimes you'll be given a blank slate, or rather a blank screen, and have the opportunity to create a persona from scratch.

Your persona is your business's personality. It's not the same thing as your product, although of course that matters: I can't be the only one who rolls my eyes at hackneyed LinkedIn career advice posts from people whose only achievement appears to be writing a book about positive thinking and yelling at people to buy it.

Your persona is how your business tells its story, a story you want others to read and hopefully share. For example, a business making really useful but fairly dull things might choose a persona based around being helpful across all walks of life, not just based on its own products; a business targeting a particular group of consumers might choose a persona designed to amuse and entertain that specific group of consumers.

The Waterstones Twitter account belonging to its Oxford Street branch is a great example of the latter: followers loved its posts so much that one of them, Victoria O'Brien, ended up marrying the man who wrote the tweets. How is that for brand engagement?

---

[8] See https://www.huffingtonpost.co.uk/2015/04/02/frankie-boyle-calls-richard-branson-mad-ct-over-global-warming_n_6990728.html

Jonathan O'Brien gave Waterstones' Twitter account a very likeable personality that was perfect for bookish types: literary, punchy and often very funny in a self-deprecating way. For example, in one tweet Waterstones said: 'Imagine your favourite book. Quick! BUY IT! BUY IT FROM WATERSTONES!' Shortly afterwards, the punchline: 'It turns out most of you already own a copy of your favourite book. We haven't thought this marketing campaign through.'[9]

It's something that's been widely copied by all kinds of brands, and, when it's done well and appropriately, it can be very successful. But it doesn't fit every kind of company. If your customers expect you to be sober and serious, then flippancy and irreverence will irritate them, not enthuse them. For example, would you want to contact a firm to discuss significant investment decisions if their online persona was that of an overly enthusiastic puppy? Are you really going to be in the mood for comedy when you're trying to Skype a key customer and your broadband's just gone down?

THE PILLARS OF A BRAND PERSONA

When you are crafting an online persona there's a bit more to it than deciding whether or not to crack the odd joke.

Marketers like to talk about 'brand pillars', which define a business's brand identity. Those pillars include:

Brand mission

This is your company's reason for existing. For example, Apple says it makes 'the best personal computers in the world'.[10] Nike says its mission is to 'bring inspiration and innovation to every athlete in the world',[11] adding that 'if you have a body, you

---

[9] See https://twitter.com/waterstonestcr/status/411515086415470592?lang=en
[10] See https://www.investopedia.com/ask/answers/042315/what-apples-current-mission-statement-and-how-does-it-differ-steve-jobs-original-ideals.asp
[11] See https://help-en-us.nike.com/app/answer/a_id/113

are an athlete'. Google promises to 'organise all the world's information and make it universally accessible and useful'.[12]

Brand values

Brand values are what your business stands for. Adidas says its values include performance, passion, integrity and diversity.[13] Adobe states that it's genuine, exceptional, innovative and involved.[14] Build-A-Bear Workshop's values include reach, learn, di-bear-sity, colla-bear-ate and cele-bear-ate.[15] Really.

Brand positioning

This is where your brand sits compared to your rivals. Greggs positions itself as a fun, carefree and irreverent no-frills food company. Apple positions itself as the tech firm for people who 'think different' from the crowd. Volvo goes for sober safety, Walt Disney for magic, Avis for trying harder than the rest.

Voice and tone

The voice and tone of your business's communications should reflect the mission, values and positioning of your brand, and do it in a way that makes people want to read and, in many cases, share what you've got to say. It should also be appropriate for and tailored to the audience you're trying to reach. As the cliché puts it, you won't reach anybody if you're trying to reach everybody.

Here is a good example of a tailored pitch: I have just backed a Kickstarter campaign for a clever laptop bag because the video pitch stood out among the tediously plinky, perky pitch videos that infest my Facebook feed every day. Fantastically bad-tempered, spectacularly foul-mouthed and very, very

---

[12] See https://www.google.com/about/our-company/
[13] See http://sustainabilityreport.adidas-group.com/en/SER2007/b/b_1.asp
[14] See https://www.adobe.com/uk/about-adobe/fast-facts.html#values
[15] See https://careersapp.buildabear.com/AboutUs.aspx

funny, it held my attention long enough to persuade me to investigate and invest in the product.[16]

The video was tailored very specifically for people who find Kickstarter pitches po-faced and annoying and worked perfectly – but it also risked turning off the kind of people who like po-faced pitches. In this case it's paid off and the project is fully funded, but it could easily have backfired too. Humour is hard, as we'll discover when we investigate some of the worst social media disasters in Chapter 9.

Content

Voice and tone is not just about what you post. It's also something that should apply to anything your social media accounts may share that's been created by others. Despite endless Twitter bios stating that retweets don't mean approval or that opinions don't necessarily reflect the views of a particular business, it's generally believed that if you share somebody else's picture, video or link without specifically criticising it, then you like it and approve of whatever sentiments are expressed in it. If it doesn't fit your brand persona – an off-colour joke from a blue-chip organisation, perhaps; a controversial post about something completely unrelated to what your business does or what your audience is interested in; or a political item when you're a thoroughly apolitical organisation – it should not be shared on your account.

BE CONSISTENT, BUT BE SENSIBLE

Branding works best when it's consistent, but it's important to bring some common sense to it too. If your business's public persona is fun and funky that's great, but if you accept and reply publicly to customer queries on social media, you need to put the customer first.

---

[16] See https://www.kickstarter.com/projects/557072737/anvanda-a-great-f-cking-bag

Virgin Trains' sexism row is a good example of how not to do it. The customer had an experience that fell short of Virgin Trains' stated mission[17] – 'to make every second you spend with us awesome ... our lovely staff make train travel something you actually look forward to' – and rather than address the issue, their response just insulted her further. Whoever posted the tweet was thinking 'how can I be funny here?', not 'how can I make this customer happy?' Many social media failures are the result of that basic mistake.

KEY TAKEAWAYS

- Every brand needs an online persona.
- Personas should be consistent across all online activities, not just social media.
- Brand pillars enable you to define your business's personality, values and tone.
- If in doubt, use common sense: what's the best way to handle this?
- Never prioritise humour over helping solve a customer's problem.

---

[17] See https://www.virgintrains.co.uk/about

5   BIG IDEAS IN SMALL SPACES

How many elephants can you fit in a Mini? The answer, of course, is four: two in the front and two in the back.

When you write for social media, you'll soon become familiar with the feeling of somehow managing to cram impossibly big things into impossibly small spaces.

Twitter's 280 character limit is probably the best known, but it's not the only social network to have maximum character counts. And even when you've got more room to stretch your literary legs, that doesn't necessarily mean you should use all of it. What's possible isn't always what's practical or useful.

You don't really need to worry about hitting the limits on Facebook or LinkedIn, where it's technically possible (and a thoroughly bad idea) to publish a post with tens of thousands of words. However, some networks are considerably more cautious and limit not just what you can post, but how much of it people can see.

Here is one enlightening statistic from 2016: 59% of links shared on social media have never been clicked by the people sharing them. People often share news based solely on what the headline or tweet says (Dewey 2016).

WHAT YOU CAN POST VS WHAT YOU SHOULD POST ON FACEBOOK, LINKEDIN AND TWITTER

Facebook may be capable of hosting long-form content, but such content doesn't do well. When the NewsWhip site evaluated the 100 most shared posts (not paid adverts) from Facebook in June 2016, the longest ones had just 24 words; the shortest got their point across in just 11 words (Corcoran 2016).

That's because Facebook shortens any post longer than about 400 characters, cutting it off mid-sentence if necessary with a 'Read More' link. If the meat of your post doesn't appear until after that point in your post, few people will ever see it.

Multiple studies suggest that the optimum length of a Facebook post is fewer than 80 characters: analysing posts by retailers, Buddy Media found that posts with fewer than 80 characters received 66 per cent more engagement than posts with more than 80 characters. It also found that posts asking questions received double the attention of posts making statements (Shearman 2011).

Another study, by advertising site AdEspresso, analysed 752,626 Facebook adverts – paid spots rather than status updates – to identify what works and what doesn't (Tate 2018). The most popular headlines were just five words long, with another 14 words of copy and then 19 words of descriptive copy. The most popular word in the ads that worked best? 'You'.

It's a similar story with LinkedIn. The sweet spot for posts is around 300 to 500 words; much longer than Facebook, but shorter than a blog post. Write as if you were writing a short article for a trade publication: don't waffle, don't produce huge blocks of densely packed text and make sure you keep your prose punchy. Bear in mind that you're writing for a professional audience and don't overstay your welcome.

Twitter has increased its character limit from 140 characters to 280, but that still doesn't give you much space. It's possible to create threaded tweets, where you reply to a tweet and then reply to your reply to your tweet and so on, but that can be cumbersome. Twitter remains best suited to the single, punchy tweet, and, while you don't have to stick to 140 characters any more, it's great if you do. Many studies suggest the optimum length of a tweet is even less: 100 characters (Lee 2016).

CHARACTER AND HASHTAG LIMITS ON OTHER SOCIAL PLATFORMS

Instagram cuts off your photo captions at 2,200 characters. However, readers only see the first three or four lines, so anything after that may be unread. That means you need to start with the strongest part of your message. You're also limited to 30 hashtags. On Twitter, that would be roughly 28 hashtags too many, but on Instagram they're used to classify, contextualise and comment on the image you're sharing so that other people will see it in search results. In this case it's good practice to use a handful of hashtags.

Pinterest is limited too: 500 characters to describe individual pins, 500 for your board description and 100 characters for your board name – although you usually only see the first 17 characters of that.

Even YouTube has limits on what you can say about your videos. Technically, you can have 100 characters for your video title, but in practice only the first 70 are shown. Similarly, you can have 5,000 characters for your description, but only the first 157 characters appear.

No matter what platform you're writing for, the trick to effective social media communication is to do more with less: you can achieve much more with a single, punchy sentence than with paragraphs of unfocused copy.

KEY TAKEAWAYS

- Don't focus on maximum post lengths. Many networks cut off content after a few lines.

- The optimum length of a social media post is much shorter than you might expect.

- The most effective word in social media is 'you'.

- Always try to do more with less.

6 HOW TO WRITE FOR SOCIAL MEDIA ON FACEBOOK, LINKEDIN, TWITTER AND THE REST

Each social network has its limits. We've already explored the physical limits, such as Twitter's maximum character limit, but others are less quantifiable, such as online readers' tendency to speed-read everything.

In this chapter we'll discover not just how much room each social network gives you, but how to make every character count.

HOW TO WRITE FOR EVERY SOCIAL NETWORK

First of all, it's always worth checking whether your chosen networks have their own style guides. For example, email marketing firm MailChimp has a very good 'Writing For Social Media' section in their *Content Style Guide*,[18] while Facebook has a guide to writing effective business adverts[19] and LinkedIn a guide to writing effective posts.[20]

We'll explore some network-specific advice in a moment, but there are some factors that apply no matter what platform you're writing for. Let's look at these first.

---

[18] See https://styleguide.mailchimp.com/writing-for-social-media/
[19] See https://www.facebook.com/business/a/creative-guide-ad-copy-tips
[20] See https://www.linkedin.com/help/linkedin/answer/47537/tips-for-writing-articles-onlinkedin?lang=en

Don't forget your brand persona

As discussed in Chapter 4, businesses with successful online marketing have a brand persona that fits them well and that's consistent across all channels. You could be fun, funky and irreverent or the voice of reason. But you need to be consistent: a witty tweet leading to a really sober web page suggests a business that is only pretending to be fun, and any content made by others that you link to or share should fit your brand persona too.

Write what your audience wants to read

It sounds obvious, I know, but not everybody does it. People are much more likely to pay attention to social media that's relevant to their interests, and to what the organisation does, rather than scattergun posting about whatever happens to be in the poster's mind. That's what personal accounts are for; business accounts need to stay focused on the things their customers want.

Don't post clickbait

Please don't make promises you won't keep. If item 3 is not going to shock us, don't tell us 'Item 3 will shock you!'; if you claim you've got a video of your MD being chased by a bear, you'd better have a video of the MD being chased by a bear. Clickbait is the internet equivalent of those local newspaper ads that used to start 'SEX! Now we've got your attention ...'.

It's also important to make sure that if you link to something, the link actually goes to that something. If you promise a blog post but link to your site's homepage, readers might decide not to go looking for it. You've gone to all that effort to get a click, and then it's been squandered.

Be clear and quick

Brevity and clarity are crucial on social media, and not just on Twitter. Many of your readers will be scrolling through posts on a smartphone, so you've got to catch their attention and keep it. Don't use jargon where plain English is better, banish buzzwords and cut, cut and cut again so that you're getting the maximum impact from the minimum amount of words.

To use our earlier example, 'Watch our MD being chased by a bear!' is much better, considerably shorter and more likely to be shared than 'Here's a video we took of our MD last year at the safari park where he got a scary surprise from a bear!'

Don't forget that posts are often read and shared on devices with very small screens, so headlines should always be short and informative. As much as I love puns, they really don't work on social media.

Don't use the passive voice

The passive voice – 'it was decided that' instead of 'we decided', for example – uses up valuable space and can suck the excitement out of even the most interesting subject. When you're writing for social media (or for any kind of media) it's a very good idea to look for weak, wishy-washy words and eliminate them.

Get to the point

Remember, social media posts are often speed-read. If it isn't immediately useful or interesting, the reader will have moved on long before you get to the point.

Don't be 'Me! Me! Me!'

The most effective social media content isn't about me, it's about you: what do you think? Do you remember these? Can you relate to this?

Don't go for the hard sell

There are exceptions to this, naturally: an irreverent social media persona can get away with the hard sell by doing it in an ironic, self-aware fashion, and it's always OK to announce genuinely good deals such as special occasion sales or limited-time offers that your readers might be interested in. But most of the time you need to be a bit more subtle than just endlessly posting sales pitches if you want people to read, let alone share, your content.

Encourage people to pass it on

Some of the best social media content is written with sharing in mind: 'Tag someone you know who'd love a hug!', 'What's the worst thing that ever happened to you at work?' or the Twitter hashtags where people have fun ruining album titles by changing one letter. Just be careful: the PR team for singer Susan Boyle created the Twitter hashtag #susanalbumparty, which was widely shared for all the wrong reasons.

One of the key tools for social media sharing is the 'at' symbol, @, especially on Twitter (although it's appearing on other social networks, such as Facebook, too). If you include @username in a post, it's sent to that post – so, for example, if you were to write '@bcs I'm really looking forward to these books!', the BCS Twitter team would see it. That enables you to talk directly to specific Twitter users, but it's important not to abuse it.

It's considered terrible etiquette to include irrelevant usernames, or to spam people by sending them unrelated content. It's also a bad idea to include too many usernames in a tweet, as that looks awfully like untargeted marketing rather than an actual desire for a conversation.

One of the worst examples of username misuse is when you disrespect someone's decision not to include a username.

That usually happens when you want to post about someone or something, but don't want that post to be seen by the subject. For example, you might want to tell people that you didn't enjoy Ricky Gervais's latest comedy special, but you don't want to post that message to Ricky Gervais himself, partly because it's rude and partly because his many followers might be nasty to you. So, you deliberately don't use @rickygervais in your message. If someone replies to you and does use @rickygervais in their message, they're effectively saying 'Hey, Ricky! Look what this person is saying about you!'

Add value

Always ask yourself, am I adding value here? Is your post going to entertain and inform people or otherwise improve their day? If you retweet somebody else's tweet, can you make it better by quoting it with a bit of commentary? Your posts or tweets should have a reason for existing.

Always credit others

This one's really important: if you're using somebody else's work, don't pass it off as yours. Share their video, not a link to it you've put on your website; include their username if you're reposting their photo, illustration or idea; if you like a joke, retweet the original, don't pretend you just thought of it. It's amazing how many companies get this one wrong.

Check yourself before you wreck yourself

Look out for typos, broken links, unclear language and anything that might fall foul of the internet police (more about them in Chapter 10). Is the tweet or post as good as it possibly can be?

Don't forget your bio

Most social networks have user profiles, usually short potted biographies that say who the poster is and link to their website. Does your bio fit your brand persona? Does it make people want to engage with you, or is it a cookie cutter bit of bland corporate speak?

Don't write one thing and put it everywhere

There are automated tools that enable you to cross-post between different social networks, so, for example, you might want every Twitter tweet to automatically appear on Facebook too. This is rarely a good idea, because what is best suited to social network A is rarely the best fit for social network B. As discussed earlier, there are big differences in the demographics of different social media platforms, and the way people use those platforms differs too.

THINGS TO THINK ABOUT WHEN YOU'RE WRITING FOR FACEBOOK

Writing for Facebook is a moving target because Facebook is constantly changing the way it works. For example, in late 2017 it announced that it was downrating content by businesses in favour of posts by individuals. Many businesses who've built their brands on Facebook saw their livelihoods flashing before their eyes.

Facebook is a platform that's undergoing constant change, and that means any strategy you have for Facebook needs to be under constant review too. What worked a month ago may not work today, and options that are available today might not be there in a few weeks.

One tool that's currently important on Facebook is the Link Preview, which appears when you post a link to an external page or article. As of early 2018, Facebook has removed the ability to choose the image thumbnail from its posting page, but you can customise what appears on Facebook by adding meta tags to your website.

Meta tags are labels that describe your content, so, for example, you might set a page title and a page description to tell search engines what your page is called and what it contains.

The key ones are OG (Open Graph) tags, and Facebook has published a guide to those tags on its Developers website.[21]

---

[21] See https://developers.facebook.com/docs/sharing/webmasters/

For example:

```
<meta property="og:title" content="Seven habits of
highly successful people"/>
```

This tells Facebook the title that should appear in its preview. You'd normally add an 'og:description' tag, which is the equivalent of the <meta name="description"> tag you would use in normal web design.

While the specifics may change, the big picture doesn't. Facebook really, really, really wants to sell you advertising. That means that the more a non-paid post appears like a marketing post, the fewer people will see it and the more likely you are to receive a message offering to boost your post – that is, show it to people – in exchange for money.

If you want to get traffic organically without paying for ads, that means avoiding sales-heavy writing and traditional 'buy now!' calls to action, and focusing instead on catchy, shareable content: shareability is a key feature of the content Facebook puts first.

There's another key consideration with Facebook, and that's whether relying on it too much is bad for your business. That is particularly applicable to businesses creating digital content and businesses where online advertising is a significant part of their revenue.

In a Twitter thread that went viral in early 2018, comedy creator Matt Klinman accused Facebook of destroying the profitability of online comedy sites. As he alleged in a subsequent interview (Aswell 2018): 'Facebook is essentially running a payola scam where you have to pay them if you want your own fans to see your content.'

He explained:

> If you run a large publishing company and you make a
> big piece of content that you feel proud of, you put it up
> on Facebook. From there, their algorithm takes over, with

no transparency. So, not only is the website not getting ad revenue they used to get, they have to pay Facebook to push it out to their own subscribers. So, Facebook gets the ad revenue from the eyeballs on the thing they are seeing, and they get revenue from the publisher. It's like if *The New York Times* had their own subscriber base, but you had to pay the paperboy for every article you wanted to see.

THINGS TO THINK ABOUT WHEN YOU'RE WRITING FOR LINKEDIN

There's more to LinkedIn than CVs and job ads. Many businesses use it to demonstrate their expertise in their sector and to position themselves as important voices on specific subjects.

LinkedIn posts begin with the writer's profile, which should have a good photograph and a 120-character description that makes you sound like the excellent person you are and fits nicely with your business's brand persona.

If you're going to be using an existing profile on behalf of your business, then you may need to make some fairly big changes to the way you present yourself and network on the site. First of all, your profile should not be a CV: it's more of a calling card, detailing your achievements and underlining why your words or videos are worth paying attention to. Think of it like the author biography on a book jacket or the potted biography of a keynote speaker at a conference. It's your greatest hits, not your whole life story.

If you wish, you can also collect endorsements from other people. For example, you might want colleagues or clients to indicate that you have skills in social media or online marketing. Best not to spend much time on this: the endorsement system is so widely misused (I've had many complete strangers endorsing me for skills I don't have) that it's largely meaningless.

Once you've got your personal page, it's time to build a company page if you don't already have one. Once again, this needs to be done with your brand persona in mind, and it should focus on your business's strengths and achievements. Keep it simple, short and focused.

The next step is to build your LinkedIn network, which may require a different approach from any networking you've previously done on the site. LinkedIn will give you some help with this by suggesting people you might know, but you'll have to do most of the legwork yourself: think about connecting with current, previous and potential clients and other industry contacts rather than everybody you've ever shared a desk with. You can contact people you don't know, but if you do, make sure you include a tailored and personal note explaining why you think they should connect with you.

Finally, you can create some content. This is done from your personal page, not your company page, and should be written specifically with your LinkedIn network in mind.

LinkedIn has very helpfully provided some insights into what works and what doesn't (Roth 2017): 'Across the world, the same formula worked to develop an audience: consistency, depth and an authentic desire to create conversations, not just content.' That means no sales pitches, and keep it fairly calm unless you're writing for a US audience: they're more responsive to excitable entrepreneurs than the rest of the world.

THINGS TO THINK ABOUT WHEN YOU'RE WRITING FOR TWITTER

For businesses, Twitter is all about two things: clicks and retweets. Clicks are when readers are inspired by your content to click on the link you've provided. Retweets are when people share your post, hopefully resulting in lots of other people clicking on the link too. Blatant sales pitches don't work very well, but you do need to sell your link a little bit: as Adweek notes (Bennett 2012): 'You might have discovered the cure for cancer, but nobody is going to care if you link it next to "this is cool".'

Be careful with hashtags, which enable people to click on a #subject and see all the tweets about it. Used wisely they can work really well, but it's #pointless #to #hashtag #everything #when the #hashtags won't link to #anything #useful. And never hijack a hashtag by using it for a tweet that isn't relevant to it, or use a hashtag without checking whether it's been used for content you don't want to be associated with.

That doesn't mean you should ignore hashtags, though. Keeping an eye on relevant ones is a good way of seeing what competitors are up to and what is important to your customers, and Twitter's trending topics show you what is currently attracting attention. Third-party services such as http://hashtagify.me make it easy to stay on top of trends and tags.

Twitter is a conversational medium, not a broadcast one. If you merely tweet links to your own content or retweet others without comment, you're not encouraging people to engage. Ask questions, run polls and show some personality and you'll get much more engagement.

KEY TAKEAWAYS

- Always strive to make your posts shorter and punchier.
- Don't make promises you won't keep.
- Be wary of Facebook: it's constantly changing how it works.
- Tailor your message and format to your audience and platform.
- Don't be 'Me! Me! Me!'.

7   HOW TO WRITE THINGS PEOPLE WANT TO SHARE

The Holy Grail of social media is shareability: posts with shareability travel far and wide to reach huge numbers of people and are prioritised by platforms such as Facebook. The more shareable the content, the more valuable it may be to your business. So how do you make content that people will want to share?

There are several approaches.

ELEVEN AND A HALF WAYS TO CREATE CONTENT PEOPLE WILL SHARE

1 Humour

This is a tough one to get right, but when a social media account does humour well it can travel far beyond its core audiences. The humorous 'beefs' between rival firms' social media accounts are a good example. Orkney Library's tongue-in-cheek wind-ups of Shetland Library have attracted tens of thousands of followers and lots of media attention,[22] and big brands get lots of coverage when they needle their rivals or get into rows with firms in completely different sectors. Examples include Taco Bell fast food vs Old Spice aftershave or Honda vs Nature Valley cereal bars. Some brands take things up a notch: in early 2018, Burger King's Twitter team managed to

---

[22] See https://www.telegraph.co.uk/news/2016/04/05/incredible-twitter-feud-between-remote-scottish-libraries-reigni/

troll President Trump and McDonalds simultaneously,[23] while also appealing to net neutrality supporters.

You don't need to pick a fight with your rivals to use humour effectively. Funny images, captions or videos do the job just as well, provided they really are funny.

2 Validation

Everybody wants to be liked by others, and sharing content that makes you seem like a good person is a good way of fuelling that basic human desire. That validation may come from being the first person to share something really interesting or entertaining, or it may come from sharing content whose message says something about the person sharing it: that they care about particular issues, or that they support particular good causes.

That doesn't mean you should fill your social media feeds with pictures of sick puppies, charity appeals or posts condemning Things That Are Bad, but if your business does good work for, or supports, particular good causes then that can be a good source of shareability – and the sharing benefits the good causes by spreading awareness of issues or appeals, so everybody wins.

3 Universality

Buzzfeed has built an entire media empire on sharable content, and much of what it posts has a universal element to it: '20 things you'll remember if you went to university in the 1990s'; '19 things only people called Julie will understand'; '17 things to do when you hate your co-worker' and so on. People love to share this kind of content and will often tag their friends in a 'did you see this? It's so you!' way. So, if you can come up with a funny list of 22 things every IT director wants to say to their suppliers, you could do very well with this approach.

---

[23] See https://www.thesun.co.uk/news/5266729/kfc-trolls-mcdonalds-donald-trump-inspired-tweet/

I am not being funny about being funny here. Security firm Kroll OnTrack got stacks of publicity every year with its list of data disasters, such as laptops in baths, laptops accidentally left on car roofs before being driven over and so on,[24] and many IT firms have found that similarly shocking lists generate good traffic.

4 Usefulness

How-to content can do very well, especially if it meets a specific customer demand or solves a common problem. If it's a really off-the-wall idea or has some element of 'wow!' to it, better still.

5 Uselessness

It can be a lot of fun to watch somebody do something really badly. A good example of that is the 2010 YouTube video by Steve from Webstaurant Store, a restaurant supplier: his Fried Gnocchi video, in which he is pelted by pasta balls while howling with laughter, has been viewed more than 3 million times (and the outtakes managed another 10,000 views).[25] His company, at the time of writing, has nearly 7,000 YouTube followers, 5,871 Twitter followers, 8,841 Instagram followers and 83,583 Facebook likes.[26] Those are extraordinary numbers for what is essentially a small B2B operation. Of course, few of those followers are likely to be customers or even potential ones, but the business is punching way above its weight in the brand awareness stakes, with very little in the way of expense or effort.

6 Informed criticism

Everybody likes a good argument, and a well-informed, well-researched takedown of somebody else's topical post can be shared widely – especially if the original poster isn't well liked.

---

[24] See https://www.ontrack.com/uk/services/data-recovery/top-10/
[25] See https://www.youtube.com/watch?v=UkXy12xVnRs
[26] See https://www.instagram.com/webstaurantstore/?hl=en

Journalists get a lot of traffic by fact-checking politicians, but it's an option for all kinds of businesses: there's no shortage of scaremongering and ill-informed nonsense churned out by celebrities, publications and some big-name brands on social media that you could correct, debunk or mock. As ever, stick to your own area of expertise and/or interest: wading into arguments that are not relevant to what you do or know about as an organisation may backfire on your business.

7 Trending topics

On services such as Twitter you can often see what topics are trending, which means they're currently attracting a lot of attention. Writing content specifically for those topics or hashtags can be a good way to get attention, but make sure it's the right attention: jumping onto a hashtag or topic that's got nothing to do with what you're posting is the equivalent of hiding unrelated keywords in your company's website: it looks bad and people are going to call you out on it.

8 Signal boosting

Signal boosting is when you use your profile to show somebody else's post to your followers, boosting their signal so it reaches more people. For example, you might retweet a customer's strange experience or unusual query and ask your followers to join the discussion, or do the reverse by sharing something you don't want to be associated with: in summer 2018, Scottish train company Scotrail's social media team was praised for telling someone sending them racist tweets, 'feel free to walk instead'.[27]

9 Really good headlines

The numbers vary from study to study, but between 59 per cent and 70 per cent of readers don't actually read the articles they share on social media. They read the headline and share

---

[27] See https://www.standard.co.uk/news/uk/feel-free-to-walk-scotrail-praised-for-reaction-to-racist-customer-a3863506.html

based solely on that. It's something that was parodied very well by *The Science Post*. Their article, 'Study: 70 per cent of Facebook users only read the headline of science stories before commenting',[28] is currently the third Google result for 'people don't read beyond the headline before sharing'. That's all the more impressive when you consider the content, which begins with this:

> 'A recent study showed that 70% of people actually never read more than the headline of a science article before commenting and sharing. Most simply see a headline they like and click share and make a comment. A recent study showed that 70% of people actually never read more than the headline of a science article before commenting and sharing. Most simply see a headline they like and click share and make a comment.'

... before continuing with multiple paragraphs of 'Lorem Ipsum' placeholder text.

A number of copywriters and social media experts have produced great guides to writing headlines for social media. For example, Neil Patel offers good advice on NeilPatel.com.[29]

10 Numbers in headlines

This is an old magazine cover trick. Don't just say you're offering tips, say you're offering 14. Odd or unusual numbers suggest serious thought: you haven't just bashed out a top 10 because you needed another four items to make the list complete. And yes, that's why this list has 11 items in it.

The trick here is to deliver on your promises: if you're promising seven cats that look like Hitler, you must provide seven cats that do indeed look like Hitler. As a study by Conductor found (Safran 2013), headlines with numbers resonate well with readers, but those readers won't thank you if the linked article

---

[28] See http://thesciencepost.com/study-70-of-facebook-commenters-only-read-the-headline/

[29] See https://neilpatel.com/blog/the-ultimate-guide-to-writing-irresistible-headlines-for-social-media/

doesn't deliver. The same study reported that numbers without superlatives ('the best', 'the greatest', etc.) often performed better than ones with them.

11 Good visuals

Text-only content is perfectly shareable, but sometimes a well-chosen image, animation or even short video clip can make the message punch that much harder.

That's partly because images and embedded videos are more noticeable compared to text – if you're scrolling through Twitter, for example, images are much more arresting than tweets containing only text, even if those tweets have better content – and partly because a great deal of social media is visual. The use of animated GIF images on Twitter is a great example of that: why post 'I agree' when you can post an animation of your favourite TV character doing a funny dance instead?

The key to images is to choose them wisely. Faces are good, but dull stock photos are so boring that there are entire parody social media accounts dedicated to them. Businesses shouldn't infringe copyright by using others' material and, as with all social media, it's important to check the background of any third-party content you post: are you absolutely certain the image you're going to use doesn't have any negative connotations?

Another kind of image, the emoji, is becoming increasingly popular too. What began as something used largely by younger users has become mainstream. With emoji, you simply use icons instead of or as well as words. So, to show you love something you might post an emoji of a love heart, or you might use an emoji of applause to show approval. This is very space efficient and works well in more irreverent settings – using emoji isn't something I would recommend for sharing controversial or potentially upsetting content.

And, of course, there's the moving image. Social networks enable you to post both live video (such as Facebook Live or the live video game streaming of YouTube's Twitch) or prerecorded video using tools such as Twitter's Periscope. Video can be very effective, especially for how-to or humorous content, but it does require more data use and can be difficult to access in areas with poor connectivity.

Nevertheless, video can be extremely effective. While some of the more excitable claims from marketing agencies should be taken with a pinch of salt, surveys from the likes of Hubspot show that, given the choice between video or text to learn about a product or service, nearly three-quarters would choose video (Hayes 2018).

11 and a half: ask them to share it

This only qualifies as half a point because it's not really about the content: it's about offering incentives to share the content, whether it's good content or not.

Many organisations run competitions where products or services are given away and the only entry requirement is for entrants to follow their account and share their post; others encourage people to share content because it's important to raise awareness of a particular issue.

Some or all of the above approaches may work for you, but it's important to remember that the key is to produce good quality content. None of the above approaches will work without it.

KEY TAKEAWAYS

- Humour works very well on social media but it's very easy to get wrong.
- People like to share content that reflects well on them.
- Universal experiences do particularly well on social media.
- Usefulness is important, but uselessness can work too.
- The most important thing is to provide good quality content.

8 READY! FIRE! AIM! THIRTEEN MISTAKES TO AVOID WHEN CREATING SOCIAL MEDIA CONTENT

Sometimes the best way to describe how to write for social media is to focus on how not to do it. You'll find that businesses whose social media channels are soundtracked by faraway church bells as tumbleweed drifts past have usually fallen into some or many of the following traps.

1 NOT HAVING A PLAN

If you don't know why you're on social media – that is, why in terms of specific objectives, not why in the vague 'we want to reach people' sense – you probably shouldn't be on social media just yet.

2 TRYING TO BE FUNNY WHEN YOU'RE NOT FUNNY

Unfortunately, the number of people who *think* they're funny is a lot bigger than the number of people who actually *are* funny. If you or your social media person are in the latter camp, then you should be grateful for your good fortune and your ability to have your followers rolling in the electronic aisles: go out there and knock 'em dead.

However, if you or your social media person are not remotely funny, then don't try to be. Nobody wants to follow the social media equivalent of an excruciatingly bad best man's speech or a stand-up comedian dying on stage.

3 EXCESSIVE SELF-PROMOTION

Unless people are following a social media account because it is purely dedicated to sales – for example, the SavyGamer feed does nothing but post details of good deals on videogames and gaming accessories – then posting lots of sales messages is counter-productive.

4 SPAMMING

Constant selling is bad enough, but organisations that pop into unrelated conversations or hashtags in order to promote their brand, product or service are even worse. It's annoying, rude and it doesn't work.

5 ONE-WAY COMMUNICATION

Some organisations see social media as another form of broadcasting, but that's not how social media works. Accounts that engage with their customers – responding to questions, joining in conversations, perhaps even retweeting their customers' posts – are more engaged and more engaging.

6 THINKING ONE SIZE FITS ALL

What tickles Twitter may not be fun on Facebook; what is impressive on Instagram may die of loneliness on LinkedIn. Posts that are not tailored to their target audience are likely to fail.

7 DOING TOO MUCH IN TOO MANY PLACES

It's better to do something really well on one or two platforms than stretch yourself too thin across every conceivable network. Chances are your target audience is more reachable on network X than on network Y.

8 IRRELEVANT CONTENT

Why are people connecting to you on social media? If it's because you're an expert in a particular kind of system, solution or situation then that's what they're expecting you to talk about. By all means, digress from time to time, but it's important to ensure that your posts are relevant to your readers or viewers.

9 LOW VALUE CONTENT

Low value content is content of little or no usefulness: it doesn't educate, inform, amuse or have any reason for existing beyond a social media person's desire to hit a particular target. As with irrelevant content, low value content is likely to drive away customers and followers.

10 POSTING TOO FREQUENTLY

There's no hard or fast rules to how often you should post, but if you're constantly demanding people's attention, you're going to quickly fall foul of the law of diminishing returns. We often find ourselves unfollowing organisations on social media because they just post too much stuff.

11 POSTING TOO RARELY

A social media presence that hasn't been updated for several months isn't going to seem very sociable, or worth following, or worth contacting with a query.

12 CAUSING OFFENCE

We'll look at this one in more detail in Chapter 10, but it's pretty self-explanatory.

13 USING SOCIAL MEDIA SOLELY FOR MARKETING

Social media is a great channel for many kinds of marketing, but it can also be a very effective recruitment platform, brand ambassador and customer service channel too.

KEY TAKEAWAYS

- It's always a good idea to have a strategy.
- Avoid posting irrelevant or low value content.
- Put quality above quantity ...
- ... but don't post too infrequently either.
- One size doesn't fit all social networks.

9   TIMING IS EVERYTHING: WHEN TO POST TO SOCIAL MEDIA

Social media isn't like email: if you post at the wrong time, your intended recipients may never see it. If you're catering for a primarily US audience, then posting at 9am UK time is shooting your social media in the foot; if you want to reach Australian early-risers, you'd better get used to posting – or, as you'll discover later in this book, scheduling your posts for – the wee small hours.

But there are sweet spots that differ from social network to social network too. Identifying the ones specific to your business, sector and audience is the work of analytics tools, which can tell you how well particular posts did compared to others, but if you're starting from scratch, you can improve your chances by posting at particular times.

It's worth noting that the various studies of effectiveness vs time are based on posting to reach all kinds of people, not specifically business audiences.[30] And it's also worth noting that other businesses will have read the same studies and will be posting at the same times, which can reduce the effectiveness somewhat.

AUSPICIOUS TIMES FOR FACEBOOK

There have been very many studies of the most effective posting times for Facebook, and the consensus is:

---

[30] See these examples: https://sproutsocial.com/insights/best-times-to-post-on-social-media/, https://blog.hootsuite.com/best-time-to-post-on-facebook-twitter-instagram/ and https://blog.bufferapp.com/best-time-to-post-on-social-media

- Don't post early in the morning or late at night.
- On weekdays, the sweet spot is 11am to 3pm ...
- ... except on Thursdays, where 1pm is the best time, not just of the day, but of the week.
- Mondays and Tuesdays are not great posting days.
- If you must post on weekends, 1pm to 2pm is the best slot and Saturdays do better than Sundays.

AUSPICIOUS TIMES FOR TWITTER

Twitter's another social network that's been analysed to death, and the results are similar – although the suggestion that early morning tweets don't work is belied by my own experience. Most of my Twitter interaction happens before I start work, with people who are commuting on public transport. However, the studies say:

- The best day is Thursday.
- The best time is noon.
- The best time slot is between noon and 3pm.
- Avoid early morning and late-night posting.

AUSPICIOUS TIMES FOR INSTAGRAM

In many ways, Instagram is the anti-matter Twitter: the best times to post to Twitter are the worst times to post to Instagram. The studies indicate that the best times are:

- any time that isn't 3pm
- Monday to Friday, but Monday most of all
- 2am, 8am and 5pm.

That reflects the fact that Instagram is a mobile platform: it's used when people are on their phones, which means travelling to and from work or education and after getting home from nights out.

AUSPICIOUS TIMES FOR LINKEDIN

As you would expect from a business-focused social network, LinkedIn posts rise or fall according to the rhythms of the business week: Fridays are for winding down and Mondays for catching up, which makes them comparatively weak days for posting. Readership tends to peak at familiar times too: on the way to work, at lunch and on the way home from work. The studies say that the best times are:

- Tuesday, Wednesday or Thursday
- 5–6pm (with the bulk of reading taking place the following morning).

AUSPICIOUS TIMES FOR OTHER FORMS OF SOCIAL MEDIA

You'll find similar recommendations for blogging (weekdays at 11am), but other networks, such as Pinterest, are more elusive: some studies say weekday evenings get the most traffic, but others point to Saturdays and Sundays as the best days for posting things people will actually read.

THE IMPORTANCE OF KNOWING YOUR AUDIENCE

As I noted in the introduction in this chapter, these numbers are averages: on average, if you post at an auspicious time you'll maximise your chances of being read and shared. However, if you are targeting a specific audience, you might find that the best times are completely different: university students keep to a very different routine from small business owners; retailers follow different rhythms from transport firms and so on. That means the guidance of others is only really there to help you get started. Experimentation and analysis will help you identify the auspicious times that work for the people you want to reach. We'll explore the abilities of analytics tools to help with that in Chapter 12.

KEY TAKEAWAYS

- Different networks have different sweet spots for maximum reach.
- Don't forget about time zones if your market isn't just the UK.
- Suggested posting times are for the average user. Your demographic may differ.
- Use monitoring tools to discover what works best for your business.

10 EVERYONE'S OFFENDED: WHEN BUSINESSES' SOCIAL MEDIA POSTS GO BADLY WRONG

One of the downsides to social media is that it's very easy to shoot yourself in the foot: a single poorly thought-out or poorly worded tweet, Facebook post or Instagram caption can quickly become a PR disaster. That's partly because the internet is a perpetual outrage machine packed with people who are desperate to be offended by the slightest thing, but it's often because businesses made some very basic mistakes.

Here are some examples of businesses who found themselves in the middle of social media firestorms.

1 KEURIG (COFFEE MACHINES)

What happened? In late 2017, the Keurig brand announced that it would pull its advertising from Fox News host Sean Hannity's show because he had given an interviewee an easy ride. Cue instant online outrage, with viral images and videos of outraged Hannity fans smashing their Keurig coffee machines. The CEO was forced to issue an apology for taking sides.[31]

The result: Outrage, boycotts, bad publicity.

The lesson learnt the hard way: Don't play politics if your brand isn't political.

---

[31] See https://www.nytimes.com/2017/11/13/business/media/keurig-hannity.html

2 H&M (RETAIL)

What happened? Take your pick. Accused of stealing music from a struggling musician in early 2018?[32] Running a campaign showing a child of colour with a T-shirt referring to him as a monkey?[33] Ongoing allegations of ripping off other people's designs?[34]

The result: Outrage, boycotts, bad publicity, withdrawal of celebrity endorsements.

The lesson learnt the hard way: Don't steal things or run ads that might appear to be racist.

3 AMERICAN APPAREL (RETAIL)

What happened? The American Apparel brand is no stranger to controversy, but its use of images of the space shuttle Challenger exploding on its Tumblr feed appeared to be an accident:[35] its social media manager was born after the disaster and thought it was a picture of fireworks.

The result: A grovelling apology after online outrage.

The lesson learnt the hard way: Don't use photos if you don't know what they are photos of.

4 US AIRWAYS (TRANSPORTATION)

What happened? A customer service agent tweeted an explicit image to an angry customer.[36] It had been tweeted to the US

---

[32] See http://www.dailymail.co.uk/news/article-5356611/H-M-accused-stealing-song-Melbourne-artist.html

[33] See https://www.washingtonpost.com/news/arts-and-entertainment/wp/2018/01/19/hm-faced-backlash-over-its-monkey-sweatshirt-ad-it-isnt-the-companys-only-controversy/

[34] See https://hypebeast.com/2017/8/hm-gosha-rubchinskiy-vestments-logo-rip-off

[35] See https://www.adweek.com/digital/american-apparel-mistakes-challenger-explosion-as-fireworks/

[36] See https://www.bbc.co.uk/news/technology-27033833

Airways account by a troll, and the agent had accidentally included a link to it while replying to a different message.

The result: Online outrage and lots of unfavourable publicity in the press.

The lesson learnt the hard way: Never, ever post a link you have not checked and checked again.

5 MIRACLE MATTRESS (BEDDING)

What happened? This is probably my favourite social media failure because it's so awful. To mark the anniversary of the 9/11 atrocity, Miracle Mattress decided to make a video featuring its 'Twin Towers sale', where staff collapsed screaming onto towers of mattresses.[37] I don't have the words to describe the spectacular, wrong-headed, tone-deaf awfulness of it.

The result: Not just online outrage and bad PR, but actual fury. The business closed its doors for a week and managed to calm the anger by admitting it was a 'national disgrace' and announcing a substantial donation to a charity for children affected by acts of terrorism.

The lesson learnt the hard way: Just ... don't.

These may seem like extreme examples, and of course they are, but you would be surprised by how many businesses attract online opprobrium for what you would think are very easily avoided mistakes: hijacking hashtags about disasters to try and sell products; posting content that's racist, sexist, transphobic or homophobic; ripping off other people's ideas or work and so on. Yet we see these things again and again and again.

---

[37] See https://www.theguardian.com/us-news/2016/sep/10/september-11-mattress-ad-backlash

I know you're made of smarter stuff, however. And that means for your business, the big risk isn't what you post, but how you respond to criticism – legitimate or otherwise. Let's discover the tricky world of angry customers and troublemaking trolls.

KEY TAKEAWAYS

- You cannot do politics or other hot-button topics without controversy.
- Social media can turn a simple marketing blunder into a massive PR disaster.
- Be vigilant for accidentally offensive imagery or content.
- Never post links without checking they go where they should.
- Don't use disasters to sell your products.

11 DO NOT FEED THE TROLLS: HOW TO HANDLE ONLINE UNPLEASANTNESS

One of the biggest downsides of social media is that it makes it much easier for people to cause trouble for your business. Sometimes that trouble is from a disgruntled customer, but sometimes that trouble can be from a critic, a prankster, campaigners for a particular cause or from trolls. Because social media is so public, how you respond to these different kinds of potential trouble can affect how other people see your organisation.

Let's look at each type in turn.

THE UNHAPPY CUSTOMER

On social media there are three kinds of unhappy customer. The first is a customer who feels that they haven't received the quality of product or service that they expected. The second is a customer who is a serial complainer, possibly of the vexatious kind: solve their problem today and they will have an equally pressing one tomorrow. And the third kind is a former customer who has been so upset by some real or perceived problem that they've decided to follow you around the internet and try to ruin your business.

The first kind of unhappy customer is the easiest to mollify: all you need to do is solve their problem. If you do that quickly, respectfully and effectively you turn an unhappy customer into a happy one and a potential negative into a positive. For many people the measure of an organisation is not how it performs when everything's going great, it's how they perform when something goes wrong.

The danger here is to mis-handle the complaint: to respond in an inappropriate way that turns a complaint into a catastrophe for your brand (remember Virgin Trains' tone-deaf sexism?). It's not enough to care about your customer. You need to be seen to care about your customer. And if in the end you can't solve their problem, a genuine apology goes a long way.

The second kind of unhappy customer is more difficult than the first because even the best of us can find ourselves losing patience with people who make repeated complaints about trivial things. Again, though, it's your response to them that really matters here. Dismiss or disparage them and it could well backfire.

There's some overlap between that kind of customer and the furious ex-customer, but with the former there's still the possibility that you can address today's problem and tomorrow's too. With the angry complainer, that is no longer an option; they've vowed to get revenge on the company that wronged them and nothing you can do will make them like you or stop them from annoying you. However, while it's possible to block that person so you won't see their messages, that won't necessarily stop anybody else from seeing their messages. As with vexatious complainers in real life, the trick is to keep your cool, be as respectful and helpful as you can and, if you can't solve their problem, apologise and shut down the conversation.

THE CRITIC

The critic isn't a customer, but they can reach your customers. The criticism may be about the way you do business, the causes your business supports, your environmental footprint, the content of your marketing or anything else connected to your business; whatever it is, the critic feels that you have a case to answer and will ask you to do so publicly.

If the criticism isn't valid, then of course you should issue a polite but emphatic denial. However, if it is valid and you can do or have already done something about it, acknowledging the issue and saying what you intend to do or what you have already done about it gives you the opportunity to turn the criticism into a positive.

You can also turn criticism into a positive even if you're not going to do anything about it. Many organisations have found themselves under pressure from special interest groups to sack employees who have criticised those groups; firms that publicly supported their staff, especially those that responded with wit or humour, often found their responses were widely shared by approving social media users. Of course, this only works if you're defending an employee who is being unfairly targeted by horrible people. Defending somebody who has done something awful isn't going to go down very well.

THE PRANKSTER

There's a long tradition of pranks, such as time-wasting letters to companies, and it was inevitable that they would make their way to social media. If you can respond in an amusing way, by all means do so. If you can't, pranksters are usually best ignored.

CAMPAIGNERS FOR A PARTICULAR CAUSE

This category is one of the most difficult ones to deal with, because in many cases campaigners occupy, or believe that they occupy, the moral high ground – they might campaign for animal welfare or environmental awareness, for particular groups' rights, or against what they consider to be unacceptable business behaviour. As with the critic, if you have taken or intend to take steps that align with what they are campaigning about, then that can become a positive PR moment.

The thing to remember here is that you're taking part in a public performance. Your replies, if you reply, will be analysed, quoted, copied and pasted. That might be to demonstrate that you're on the campaigners' side, or to demonstrate that you're the baddies in this particular situation. That means it's important to tread carefully and to pay particular attention to the risk of deliberate or accidental misinterpretation. Once again, dismissing or disparaging people's concerns is likely to be spun against you.

It's also important to identify whether you're dealing with a genuinely concerned individual or group, or if you're being targeted by trolls.

TROLLS

In legend, trolls are monsters that live under bridges and try to eat goats trying to cross those bridges. Online, trolls are monsters that annoy people trying to get on with their life or their jobs.

Trolls are not customers with issues to solve or genuine critics. Trolling is targeted harassment, and many legal experts argue that your organisation has a duty of care to protect employees from such harassment. The quickest way to silence a troll is to mute or block their account, but, unfortunately, they often return with another account and pick up from where they left off. In some cases, you may even need to call the police.

Trolls can target any business, but they are particularly prevalent where businesses work in controversial fields or where businesses support certain good causes. Engaging with them is like what Mark Twain reportedly said about wrestling with pigs: you just get dirty, and the pig enjoys it.

KEY TAKEAWAYS

- Don't assume all complaints are vexatious. Some are from genuine customers.
- Don't be defensive or dismissive of customers, no matter how irritating they may be.

- Responding well to criticism can enable you to show your business in a positive light.

- Tread carefully around campaigners, who will circulate any response you make.

- Don't wrestle with a troll.

12 TOOLS OF THE TRADE: FROM APPS TO ANALYTICS

There are many tools that can help you to manage and analyse your social media presence. They are probably overkill for a simple social media account, but they can be very valuable for managing, monitoring and evaluating bigger social media operations.

POST SCHEDULERS

Social media may operate 24/7, but you don't – so, if you're catering for audiences around the world, a social media post scheduler is going to be a real boon. As the name suggests, it enables you to write posts in advance and specify when they should go online, so you can be entertaining or enlightening your followers while you're happily tucked up in bed.

There is a variety of scheduling tools, from content management systems such as WordPress, to social media apps such as Buffer. Some apps enable you to share the same content across multiple social networks too; although, as discussed in previous chapters, that's not necessarily a good idea. It's better to look for a scheduler that supports multiple networks but doesn't require you to send the same content to each one.

ANALYTICS

Many of the big-name platforms provide analytics tools that enable you to analyse your social media performance; if you've used Google's ad-tracking tools, you'll already have a good idea of what to expect. Facebook and Twitter have similarly comprehensive tools.

The specifics differ per platform, but generally they enable you to see what audience you're reaching, what content is doing the best job of reaching them and what the audience does when it accesses your content. That information is invaluable.

There are many third-party analytics solutions, but it's worth checking out the platforms' own products first. For example, Facebook's own Analytics tool is both free and powerful. It provides data on key metrics, such as unique users, new users and user demographics, user retention and so on, and it's extensively customisable so that you can focus on the data that's most valuable to you.

SOCIAL MEDIA DASHBOARDS

A dashboard enables you to get a bird's eye view of your social media: the accounts you're interested in, the people talking about you, your followers and retweets and anything else that might be useful.

Many dashboards combine post scheduling and analysis tools in a single package; so, for example, Buffer enables you not just to schedule posts across the different networks, but also to see how well they have performed and what content has performed best.

Some dashboards are incredibly flexible. One of the best-known dashboards, Hootsuite, connects to 35 different social networks and delivers scheduling, trend and topic monitoring, content creation and analytics, and it's also available in team-based versions for larger organisations.

Such online apps come at a price, but it's less than you might think; for example, the single user version of Hootsuite is currently, at the time of writing, £16 per month for unlimited scheduling across 10 social networks. For teams, pricing starts at £80 per month for three users. Buffer is similar: its Small Business Plan is $99 for 25 accounts, five team members and a scheduling queue of up to 2,000 posts at any time.

Most dashboard services also offer individual accounts and trial accounts, which enable you to test the services before committing to spending any money.

KEY TAKEAWAYS

- Post scheduling is great for global reach. Look for services that span multiple networks.

- Many social networks provide surprisingly good analytics tools for free.

- Social media dashboards combine posting, scheduling and analytics in one place.

- Dashboards cost money, but not as much money as you might expect.

- Take advantage of personal or trial accounts to test-drive paid services.

AFTERWORD

For most businesses, social media is nothing new; it's just another channel for marketing or for customer service. However, while the basics of social media communication will not change, the specifics will.

In a tweet that went viral, Twitter user @actioncookbook expertly parodied Twitter's apparent enthusiasm for making unpopular changes. To date it has received 30,000 likes and been retweeted 20,000 times.[38]

USERS: you're alienating the people who actually use your product

TWITTER: likes are now florps

USERS: what

TWITTER: timeline goes sideways

It's funny because it's true, sometimes frustratingly so. For example, in August 2018, Twitter shut down some of the application programming interfaces (APIs) that third-party apps and services such as Tweetbot and Twitteriffic used to provide social media monitoring data to individuals and organisations. Features that many people had come to rely upon simply disappeared. Shorn of key features, some of the apps may disappear too.

---

[38] See https://twitter.com/actioncookbook/status/684515262712967170?lang=en

One reason social media keeps changing is because it's very competitive. The big networks need to grow both in terms of user numbers and in user engagement, and in order to do that they keep changing their product offerings and experimenting with different ways of doing things. At the time of writing, Facebook is currently updating its mobile app every single week, and we can't say with confidence that a feature that's in the app today will still be there in a week, let alone a year. As I wrote this paragraph, I received a Facebook notification that it was changing the way companies' Facebook Pages would be displayed.

Such changes are constant, and largely irrelevant. Effective communication is all about getting the right information to the right people at the right time using the right channel. It doesn't matter if it's on Twitter or Facebook, or if likes really do become florps. It's your message that matters, not the messenger.

Happy posting.

APPENDIX:
THE TOP ELEVEN SOCIAL NETWORKS PEOPLE ARE ACTUALLY USING

There are dozens of social networks out there, but the biggest ones tend to be really, really big. That's because of something called the network effect: you go where the people you want to connect with are. So, beyond a certain size, the big sites keep getting bigger while smaller rivals with lesser network effects find it hard to catch up. However, what is big today might not be big tomorrow. For example, in late 2016 the short-video social network Vine had over 200 monthly active users; in January 2017 its owner, Twitter, shut it down.

At the time of writing, these are the top 11 social networks people are actually using. Some of the estimated user numbers are on the high side; for example, the photo sharing network Flickr has been in deep decline for some years now, and its estimated 90 million active users seems high. You will generally find that the networks doing very well can't wait to tell you how many active users they have; the ones that are not doing so well are much more secretive.

FACEBOOK: 2.2 BILLION MONTHLY ACTIVE USERS[39]

Facebook isn't just a social network. It's changing the world, for good and ill – and its demographic is changing too. It's expected that 700,000 UK teenagers and young adults will quit the service in 2018 while its popularity among the over 55s surges.[40]

---

[39] See https://newsroom.fb.com/company-info/
[40] See https://www.theguardian.com/technology/2018/feb/12/is-facebook-for-old-people-over-55s-flock-in-as-the-young-leave

YOUTUBE: 1.5 BILLION MONTHLY ACTIVE USERS[41]

You might not think of YouTube as a social network, but its content is entirely created and commented on by its users. The fastest growing segments of YouTube's ever-growing audience are currently people 35-plus and 55-plus.[42]

INSTAGRAM: 800 MILLION MONTHLY ACTIVE USERS[43]

Instagram is now part of Facebook, but its demographic skews considerably younger than the mothership. It's all about sharing photos and videos and works particularly well for businesses targeting young, image- and fashion-conscious consumers.

TWITTER: 330 MILLION MONTHLY ACTIVE USERS[44]

Twitter is famous for two things: brevity and bots. The former is its 280 character limit (formerly 140), which encourages brief messages. The latter are the fake followers and automated accounts that make some topics and organisations appear more popular than they actually are, and which mean the active user numbers are probably overly generous.

REDDIT: 250 MILLION MONTHLY ACTIVE USERS[45]

Reddit is often described as the worst of the internet: it's a relatively unregulated space where people can set up discussion areas on any conceivable subject, and some of those subjects have been awful or even illegal. However, it's also where people such as Barack Obama and Bill Gates come to do AMA (ask me anything) interviews and is the fourth most

---

[41] See https://www.youtube.com/intl/en-GB/yt/about/press/
[42] See http://mediakix.com/2017/03/youtube-user-statistics-demographics-for-marketers/#gs.Ud=QwU0
[43] See https://instagram-press.com
[44] See https://www.statista.com/statistics/282087/number-of-monthly-active-twitter-users/
[45] See https://en.wikipedia.org/wiki/Reddit

visited website in America (it's number 8 worldwide, according to Alexa Internet[46]). Its demographics are very American (56 per cent), very male (69 per cent) and very young (68 per cent between 18 and 29).

ASK.FM: 215 MILLION MONTHLY ACTIVE USERS[47]

Ask.fm is an odd one: it's where people can ask other people questions, usually pseudonymously, and in 2013 many UK advertisers pulled their campaigns from the site when it was associated with teenage bullying and implicated in a schoolgirl's suicide. It's changed ownership since then – it's now owned by Ask.com and based in Dublin, where it liaises with child protection services – but it remains a primarily teenage concern.

PINTEREST: 200 MILLION MONTHLY ACTIVE USERS[48]

Pinterest is where millions of people share content by pinning it to virtual boards and, as you might expect, that means it's been embraced by businesses working in visual media such as crafts, fashion, design and anything else where a picture paints a thousand words. It's female dominated – some studies suggest as many as 81 per cent of its users are women – and women are more active too; men are responsible for just 7 per cent of the pins on the network[49]. Among millennials it's as popular as Instagram.

GOOGLE+: 111 MILLION MONTHLY ACTIVE USERS[50]

Google+ was supposed to be a Facebook killer, but, according to statistics site Statista, its share of the social network market in the UK fell from 0.2 per cent in March 2015 to less

---

[46] See https://www.alexa.com/siteinfo/reddit.com
[47] See https://medium.com/@askfm/a-new-take-on-your-favorite-platform-73910fd7564a
[48] See https://business.pinterest.com/en/audience-demographics-user-stats
[49] See https://www.omnicoreagency.com/pinterest-statistics/
[50] See https://www.statista.com/statistics/280422/social-networks-market-share-held-by-google-in-the-united-kingdom-uk/

REFERENCES

Aswell, Sarah (2018) *How Facebook is killing comedy*. Vulture. Available from: http://www.vulture.com/2018/02/how-facebook-is-killing-comedy.html [accessed 23 August 2018].

Bennett, Shea (2012) *How to write the perfect tweet*. Adweek. Available from: https://www.adweek.com/digital/the-perfect-tweet/3/ [accessed 23 August 2018].

nnan, Bridget (2017) *When it comes to marketing, women are original social network*. Forbes. https://www.forbes.com/sites/etbrennan/2017/08/01/when-it-comes-to-marketing-en-are-the-original-social-network/#3783d1f0596d sed 23 August 2018].

n, Liam (2016) *What's the perfect length of a Facebook* wsWhip. Available from: http://www.newswhip. /07/perfect-length-of-a-facebook-post/ [accessed 2018].

7) *UK public are 'glued to smartphones' as device hes new heights*. Deloitte. Available from: https:// e.com/uk/en/pages/press-releases/articles/ d-to-smartphones.html [accessed 23 August

16) *6 in 10 of you will share this link without depressing study says*. The Washington https://www.washingtonpost.com/news/ 016/06/16/six-in-10-of-you-will-share-eading-it-according-to-a-new-and-cessed 23 August 2018].

than 0.05 per cent in July 2017, making it effectively irrelevant to businesses. It's widely seen as a disaster, but it does have loyal users in fields such as landscape photography and board games. However, its glory days are far in the past.

LINKEDIN: 106 MILLION MONTHLY ACTIVE USERS[51]

LinkedIn is an interesting one: that figure is for Q3 2016, last time LinkedIn published user numbers. Many p suggest that the business-focused network's current n are much, much lower: while it has more than half members, they use the site much less frequently social media users do.

TUMBLR: FEWER THAN 100 MILLION M ACTIVE USERS[52]

Tumblr is a cross between a bloggir sharing service: some people use i photos they feel mean something massively young, with nearly 50 from the 16 to 24 age group younger users too.

FLICKR: 90 MILLION

Flickr is a photo sh for photographer owner, Yahoo, F its casual ph people who have beer

[51] See http
[52] See http://w
2013-5?IR=T
[53] See https://expand

Hayes, Adam (2018) *The state of video marketing in 2018*. HubSpot. Available at: https://blog.hubspot.com/marketing/state-of-video-marketing-new-data [accessed 23 August 2018].

Lee, Kevan (2016) *Infographic: the optimal length for every social media update and more*. Buffer Social. Available at: https://blog.bufferapp.com/optimal-length-social-media [accessed 23 August 2018].

Leslie, Jennifer (2018) *55 social media marketing stats and facts for 2018*. Infusionsoft. Available from: https://www.infusionsoft.com/business-success-blog/marketing/social-media/cost-social-media-marketing-stats-and-facts [accessed 23 August 2018].

McCarthy, John (2015) *Facebook influences over half of shoppers says DigitalLBi's Connected Commerce report*. The Drum. Available from: http://www.thedrum.com/news/2015/04/24/facebook-influences-over-half-shoppers-says-digitaslbi-s-connected-commerce-report [accessed 23 August 2018].

Petersen, Rob (2015) *15 powerful facts to guide your social media strategy*. BarnRaisers. Available at: http://barnraisersllc.com/tag/business-strategy/page/2/ [accessed 23 August 2018].

Roth, Daniel (2017) *LinkedIn top voices 2017: meet the all-stars driving today's professional conversations*. LinkedIn. Available at: https://www.linkedin.com/pulse/linkedin-top-voices-2017-must-know-people-inspiring-todays-roth/ [accessed 23 August 2018].

Safran, Nathan (2013) *5 data insights into the headlines readers click*. Moz.com. Available at: https://moz.com/blog/5-data-insights-into-the-headlines-readers-click [accessed 23 August 2018].

Shearman, Sarah (2011) *Retailers should reduce their Facebook posts, says Buddy Media*. Campaign. Available at: https://www.campaignlive.co.uk/article/retailers-reduce-facebook-posts-says-buddy-media/1091867 [accessed 23 August 2018].

Stainmetz, Katy (2017) *Does tweeting at companies really work? Time* magazine. Available at: http://time.com/4894182/twitter-company-complaints/ [accessed 23 August 2018].

Tate, Andrew (2018) *We analyzed 752,626 Facebook ads, and here's what we learned (2018 update)*. AdEspresso. Available at: https://adespresso.com/blog/we-analyzed-37259-facebook-ads-and-heres-what-we-learned/ [accessed 23 August 2018].

Vaughan, Pamela (2017) *72 per cent of people who complain on Twitter expect a response within an hour*. Hubspot. Available at: https://blog.hubspot.com/marketing/twitter-response-time-data [accessed 23 August 2018].

Wagner, Kurt (2017) *How many people use Twitter every day?* Recode.net. Available at: https://www.recode.net/2017/7/27/16049334/twitter-daily-active-users-dau-growth-q2-earnings-2017 [accessed 23 August 2018].

York, Alex (2017) *Social media demographics to inform a better segmentation strategy*. Sproutsocial. Available at: https://sproutsocial.com/insights/new-social-media-demographics/ [accessed 23 August 2018].

INDEX

CPSIA information can be obtained
at www.ICGtesting.com
Printed in the USA
FFHW010653220719
53804626-59482FF

9 781780 174501